To

_____

From

_____

Date

_____

See the Wind, Mommy

See the Wind, Mommy

Sensing God's Presence through the Lives of Your Children

Marsha Crockett

Baker Books

A Division of Baker Book House Co
Grand Rapids, Michigan 49516

Published by Baker Books
a division of Baker Book House Company
P.O. Box 6287, Grand Rapids, MI 49516-6287

Printed in the United States of America

Library of Congress Cataloging-in-Publication Data

Crockett, Marsha, 1957–
   See the wind, Mommy : sensing God's presence through the lives of your children / Marsha Crockett.
      p.   cm.
   Includes bibliographical references.
   ISBN 0-8010-1100-0 (cloth)
    1. Mothers—Religious life. 2. Children—Religious Life. 3. Presence of God. 4. Spiritual life—Christianity. I. Title.
BV4529.C76   1996
242'.6431—dc20   95-52262

Dedicated to
My Little Women,
Megan Elizabeth and Amy Jo
My two most brilliantly crafted gifts from God

Contents

Acknowledgments

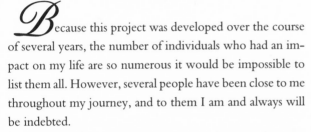

*B*ecause this project was developed over the course of several years, the number of individuals who had an impact on my life are so numerous it would be impossible to list them all. However, several people have been close to me throughout my journey, and to them I am and always will be indebted.

The members of the Tempe Christian Writers' Group have been invaluable to me as a writer and in keeping me on track with what God wants me to do with my writing. Not only has their level of competence and professionalism assisted me in developing my craft, but they have been supreme examples for giving my best to the Lord.

My parents, Lee and Shirley McQuinn, gave me not only the roots and the wings I needed to make it in this world but also a gift more precious than life itself; it was in the

*Acknowledg-
ments*

home where I grew up that they showed me who God is and that he is a God for me.

Finally, my husband John lovingly challenges me, confronts me, and enables me to grow and give and love our Lord in the manner in which I am designed to do. Thanks for putting up with the early morning hours and pages of rough draft I made you endure. I could never be the mother I am without your being the father you are to our girls. It's an incredible journey and I'm lavishly blessed to walk it with you.

How to Use this Book

*T*his is not only a book to be read; it is also a book to be acted on. It is based on the discoveries about God I made during my mothering years. All that is written here is to help you listen to God's message for you as you discover his will.

Each chapter is set up to comprise one week's devotions. The readings for each week are words taken from my journals of my days with my small daughters at home. I've attempted to keep them as a record of my own thoughts rather than use them to preach to the reader. I pray the words will encourage you to start your own journal if you've not done so before. I offer the book to you friend to friend.

The key verse and key thought for each day are designed to start your thinking and can be used as springboards for your journal if you wish to keep one.

Following are some guidelines and suggestions to help you get the most from your experience with this book:

13

1. Pray for God's leading as you read and study. He may have a message ready for you each day if you are open to receive it.

2. Remember, God is pleased with your desire, not your words, to meet him in your daily routines. Whether you talk to him from your heart or write, don't be concerned whether you use proper grammar or say it just right. God knows your heart. I like to pray the prayer of Moses in Exodus 33:13, 14, 17 before I begin my time with God. It tells him my desire, and it reassures me of his desire toward me: "If you are pleased with me, teach me your ways so I may know you and continue to find favor with you. . . . The LORD replied, 'My Presence will go with you, and I will give you rest. . . . I will do the very thing you have asked, because I am pleased with you and I know you by name.'"

You may want to choose your own verse to pray, or simply talk to God in your own words.

3. If you decide to keep a journal, use a separate notebook. Write what comes to mind following your daily devotional study or anytime during the day. There is a blank page at the end of each chapter so you can record your discoveries and reactions. You will find suggestions throughout this book for using a journal to list God's gifts, track prayer requests, or write your own prayers.

4. As you read the key verse for the day, ask God what he's saying to you. Share your thoughts with him as well. In most cases it will be beneficial to read the verses preceding and following the key verse. If you don't understand the passage, ask him for wisdom. James 1:5 says, "If any of you lacks wisdom, he should ask God, who gives generously to all without finding fault, and it will be given to him."

5. The key thought is written briefly and is intended to spark your own further thinking. Take time to explore the idea with God. If after you read the key verse God leads you in a different direction from the key thought, then go where he leads.

6. The Scripture selections for the week are by no means the entire realm of study on each subject. Take time, as it is given, to search the Scriptures on your own. Use a concordance or cross references in your Bible.

7. On the last day of each week's study is a prayer that has come out of my own journey. Use this day to focus on communication through prayer. You may want to write your own prayers and record God's responses. Much about praying lies in the listening and waiting. Don't feel obligated to ramble on to God. Take a deep breath and let him speak to you, love you, heal you.

8. In the "To Do" section are three or four ideas to put your discoveries into practice. Acting on what God has given

you will take you to new levels of understanding. James 1:22 says, "Do not merely listen to the word, and so deceive yourselves. Do what it says."

My prayer as you begin this discovery process is found in Ephesians 3:16–19:

> I pray that out of his glorious riches he may strengthen you with power through his Spirit in your inner being, so that Christ may dwell in your hearts through faith. And I pray that you, being rooted and established in love, may have power, together with all the saints, to grasp how wide and long and high and deep is the love of Christ, and to know this love that surpasses knowledge—that you may be filled to the measure of all the fullness of God.

Introduction

*M*otherhood. Some days I just want out! Every mother with young children entertains such thoughts at one time or another. I remember such a day when I wanted no more whining, no more demands, no more ingratitude. I especially wanted no more Vaseline smeared on the bathroom wall "to make it look shiny." I really could live without Crayola on my Linoleum. And I didn't need any more pink bubble gum on my black suede shoes.

I viewed a close relationship with God as something similar to a mirage in the desert. It always seemed to be just beyond my grasp, melting into nothing more than a watered down hope for something better, deeper, more real than what I held. Must I wait until the kids were older before I could really get to know God? After all, it seemed my children were my biggest obstacles to maintaining that relationship. I simply didn't have the energy or the know-how to switch gears between dirty diapers and daily devotions.

17

But with God's prodding, I began to realize he had placed my children between him and me as stepping stones, not obstacles to be hurdled.

I needed my spiritual growth to shake hands with my growth as a mother, not slap it in the face. That's when I called to God, "Save me from these kids!" Although I intended it as a hypothetical exclamation, he answered me. Straight from the heart of my heavenly Father to me, his daughter, came three simple words: "Be like them."

This realization freed me not only to see my children in a different light but to love them more deeply. I no longer say, "I'm serving Jesus *in spite* of the fact I have children." Now I say, "I'm learning to love Jesus more *because* my children lead the way."

Every woman must come to her own realization of what God has planned for her. Every journey leads down a different road. Every discovery process is unique. But when we stoop down to love our children, we're close enough to hear God's very heartbeat. When we look into the eyes of our children, we meet God face to face. It's during those moments of motherhood that God not only speaks to us but also teaches us all over again to become like a little child—his child.

1

See the Wind, Mommy

Sensing God's Presence

To live in the presence of God . . . is to live with purity of heart, with simplemindedness. . . . That, indeed demands a choice, a decision and great courage.

Henri Nouwen

*A*s the Arizona summer winds drove dust across the desert, I grumbled at the tiny drifts accumulating on my clean-swept patio. But my toddling daughter Amy let me in on a secret about the wind. Squealing with glee, she said, "See da win', Mommy!" I watched, enraptured by her sheer delight. She turned to feel the full force of the breeze on her little face and laughed aloud. Her baby-fine hair leapt up and around to brush her rosy cheeks with softness. She squinted her eyes as if to find the source of the power blowing her way.

Watching the limbs of the tree overhead bow and wave, she waved her arms in a neighborly reply. She bobbed up and down with the bend of her knees, dancing with the daisies in the flower bed. With each new discovery, she called to me, "See, Mommy!"

How could I have been so blind to such a marvel? With each call from Amy to see, God opened my eyes to this realization: If I had missed the joy of seeing the wind, what else had escaped my vision? I knew then God wanted to reveal his wonders to me, but I did not have the proper focus in my life.

In my day-to-day living it's easy to allow insignificant problems to get between me and God. The down-and-dirty details of living often leave me with tunnel vision. All I can see some days are a sink full of dishes to be washed, a basket filled with clothes to be folded, and two little girls wanting to be fed again. How can I see God in the routine ruts I drag my wheels through each day? My Bible heroes met God in miraculous ways. It would be a snap to see the living God

and talk with him if I experienced some of that "old-time religion."

I made a point to take a second look at these heroes. But this time I'd look with my new focus on God in the ordinary ways of life. Yes, their lives and stories did look different from those I had learned about in Sunday school as a child. When Moses met God in the burning bush, he was simply trying to keep a flock of sheep in line for his father-in-law. When Paul fell to his knees blinded by the heavenly light, he was commuting to work. Jesus called many of his apostles while they worked on the job (fishing, collecting taxes).

Why should it be any different for me? I must open my eyes to God's presence rather than bemoan my life as one filled with routine drudgery. I want to see God when I'm looking at the dirty dishes or wondering where my day has gone, or when I'm trying to meet a deadline. Maybe then I can begin to dance with the daisies, too.

DAY ONE

Key Verse: Exodus 33:13, 14 If you are pleased with me, teach me your ways so I may know you and continue to find favor with you. . . . The LORD replied, "My Presence will go with you, and I will give you rest."

Key Thought: How can I dance with the daisies when I'm drowning in dirty dishes?

DAY TWO

Key Verse: Isaiah 30:15 (KJV) Thus saith the LORD . . . In returning and rest shall ye be saved; in quietness and confidence shall be your strength.

Key Thought: What key words in this verse can help me stop and sense God's presence and strength?

DAY THREE

Key Verse: Jeremiah 23:23–24 "Am I only a God nearby," declares the LORD, "and not a God far away? Can anyone hide in secret places so that I cannot see him? . . . Do not I fill heaven and earth?" declares the LORD.

Key Thought: When have I felt God's presence in my life, and what did I learn from that experience?

DAY FOUR

Key Verses: listed below in key thought

Key Thought: The verses below reveal five ways to sense God's presence. Which way do I experience most often? Which way is the most difficult for me? John 14:7–9; Romans 1:20; 2:13, 15; 15:4; 2 Corinthians 3:2, 3.

See the Wind, Mommy

25

DAY FIVE

Key Verse: Acts 17:25, 27 He himself gives all men life and breath and everything else . . . God did this so that men would seek him and perhaps reach out for him and find him, though he is not far from each one of us.

Key Thought: What hinders me from sensing God's presence?

DAY SIX

Key Verse: James 4:8, 10 Come near to God and he will come near to you. . . . Humble yourselves before the LORD and he will lift you up.

Key Thought: Why should I seek God's presence?

DAY SEVEN

Father who sees the wind,

    Open my eyes to see the wonders of life

        as only a child can see.

    Open my heart to your message, your thoughts,

        your ways.

    Open my hands to receive all these marvels.

    Let your presence go with me to give me your rest.

Amen.

To Do

1. Use your time wisely for God's purposes. Rather than fight the traffic, use the time to sing a song of praise, repeat a memorized Bible verse, pray for your family.

2. Explore nature with your children. Give them two or three things to look for (a striped rock, a bug, two different leaves, etc.) and see what they discover right in your own backyard. Think about a spiritual truth that might be applied to the objects they find.

3. Honor the Sabbath, God's day of rest. Let go of routine chores. Take joy in the gifts God gives, especially the people you love.

My Turn

*See the
Wind,
Mommy*

MY TURN

2

A Radish of Joy
Knowing the Joy of the Lord

> *Never let anything so fill you with sorrow as to make you forget the joy of Christ risen.*
>
> Mother Teresa

*T*he cold weather had kept us cooped up too long. I could barely keep myself motivated to straighten the house, let alone give it a good cleaning. So at the first signs of warming, my daughters and I ventured outside to dig up a small plot of ground for a spring vegetable garden.

29

It felt good to participate in God's re-creation. We began to plant corn, lettuce, peas, and broccoli. We placed the ever-so-tiny seeds into little dirt ditches and covered them over with more dirt. As expected, within a few weeks the seeds sprouted. But as they grew, we noticed one plant in the broccoli patch that appeared to be different from the others. The leaves were rounder and darker, the stem thicker. We watched the little plant with great interest and wondered what made this sprouting life so unusual.

One day I put my face down close to the plant to examine it more carefully. Poking a finger at the dirt, I noticed a reddish tinge underneath and dug a bit further. "A radish!" I yelled to my girls to come see. They couldn't believe this wonderful "treasure" in our broccoli patch. We quickly washed it off, sliced the little thing into equal parts, and nibbled on God's gift like three giggling bunnies. Here was unexpected joy in the midst of my winter doldrums.

Scripture is filled with the paradox of joy from heartache. Consider the following "seeds of sorrow" and the joyful crops they produced. When Shadrach, Meshach, and Abednego stood in the flaming furnace, an entire nation found God and worshiped him (Dan. 3:16–30). When Hannah relinquished her only son to an old priest, God's prophet was born (1 Sam. 1:27–28). When Paul was chained in prison, salvation came to his captors (Acts 16:23–34). And when

A Radish of Joy

Jesus breathed his last breath on the cross, humanity took its first breath of freedom from sin (Mark 15:37–39).

So when I'm depressed over the trivialities of life or the heavier burdens and heartaches, I'll look for God's radish of joy in my ordinary broccoli patch of life. And when I see that bud, I'll marvel, as did David, at the good gifts God has given to me. "You will fill me with joy in your presence, with eternal pleasures at your right hand" (Ps. 16:11).

DAY ONE

Key Verse: Psalm 126:5–6 Those who sow in tears will reap with songs of joy. He who goes out weeping, carrying seed to sow, will return with songs of joy, carrying sheaves with him.

Key Thought: What things in my life keep me from harvesting God's gifts of joy?

DAY TWO

Key Verse: James 1:2–4 Consider it pure joy . . . whenever you face trials of many kinds, because you know that the testing of your faith develops perseverance. Perseverance must finish its work so that you may be mature and complete, not lacking anything.

Key Thought: How can I be joyful while dealing with my problems?

DAY THREE

Key Verse: 2 Corinthians 4:8–9 We are hard pressed on every side, but not crushed; perplexed, but not in despair; persecuted, but not abandoned; struck down, but not destroyed.

Key Thought: How do these verses relate to finding joy in sorrow?

DAY FOUR

Key Verse: Matthew 5:11–12 Blessed are you when people insult you, persecute you and falsely say all kinds of evil against you because of me. Rejoice and be glad, because great is your reward in heaven.

Key Thought: I can experience joy in the midst of my sorrow, because God gives me hope.

DAY FIVE

Key Verse: 1 Peter 4:12–13 Do not be surprised at the painful trial you are suffering, as though something strange were happening to you. But rejoice that you participate in the sufferings of Christ, so that you may be overjoyed when his glory is revealed.

Key Thought: When I'm discouraged or depressed by my circumstances, I will stop to consider how God revealed his glory through Christ's suffering.

DAY SIX

Key Verse: 2 Corinthians 5:17 Therefore, if anyone is in Christ, he is a new creation; the old has gone, the new has come!

Key Thought: How can God's gift of joy make me a new creation?

DAY SEVEN

Father of joyful surprises,
I've let my heart become cluttered again
    with boredom and bad moods.
But when I dig through all the self-pity,
    I find you've remained with me.
You promised never to leave me, but for some reason,
    I'm always surprised—joyfully surprised—to see
    it's not what I plant but what you create in me that's
    sprouting up to fill me with joy.

Amen.

TO DO

1. Take time early in the morning to give God your sorrows, disappointments, or sadness that you hide or simply cannot explain. Use a notebook to start a

prayer journal to record these thoughts. Watch for God's gift of joy to sprout up in the endeavor.

A Radish of Joy

2. As you clean the house or empty the trash or drive to work, reflect on God's ability to clean up your heart and make it fertile for his presence and his joy.

3. For every problem or sorrow you deal with today, stop to consider the good gifts from God. Include the list in your journal.

4. Plant seeds with your children. (Herbs grow in a cup or pot any time of the year.)

MY TURN

A Radish of Joy

3

Fish Bubbles and Guinea Pig Chatter

Finding a Heart of Praise

> *The World is a hidden object puzzle. It is mystery upon invisible mystery and infinite layers of holiness. It is God's presence hidden among the leaves.*
>
> Sue Monk Kidd

It was one of those days where boredom became my bedfellow. I didn't want to do anything, be bothered by any-

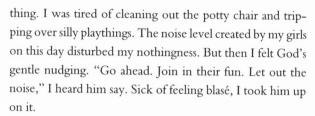

thing. I was tired of cleaning out the potty chair and tripping over silly playthings. The noise level created by my girls on this day disturbed my nothingness. But then I felt God's gentle nudging. "Go ahead. Join in their fun. Let out the noise," I heard him say. Sick of feeling blasé, I took him up on it.

I called the kids into the kitchen. "Here," I said, handing two pan lids to Megan. "And here," I added, giving Amy a little pot and a wooden spoon. I took hold of a plastic kitchen funnel. I didn't need to tell them what to do. I opened up the windows and we were off to "let out the noise."

With homemade cymbals and drum and horn, we paraded around Kitchen Circle and onto Family Room Freeway. We marched down Living Room Lane and came to a happy stop on Dining Room Drive. Quickly we all switched instruments and did it again and again until we were too tired to bang or march or blow the funnel horn anymore.

It did feel good, and I knew God was having a great belly laugh along with us. Whenever I open my window of praise, God airs out my musty soul. He dusts the corners of my mind from the tangled webs of bad moods and stale thoughts. I feel fresh and revived and ready to praise him in a new and joyful way.

*Fish
Bubbles
and
Guinea
Pig
Chatter*

*Fish
Bubbles
and
Guinea
Pig
Chatter*

But how can I keep that momentum of praise? By becoming a child, of course! By holding as precious the simple things in my life, by reveling in "every good gift and perfect gift . . . coming down from the Father of the heavenly lights" (James 1:17).

"Easy for you to say," a friend once argued. "You don't know how bad I have it. It's impossible to remain thankful and positive in the middle of all this." She said it half jokingly. But she may have a point, I thought, as I heard her four boys in the background while we chatted on the phone.

We did agree on one thing: It isn't the big problems that pull us down. In fact, most people naturally turn to God during crises. It's the humdrum, never-ending, thankless job that does me in. That's when I need help.

Consider the joy of a child. What is it that really delights children? Don't they love to play in the water, bake cookies, pet a kitten, play dress up, or run a race? So praise God as little children. Praise him and thank him for the small gifts of life.

Now, there's a challenge! Can I find praise in my perpetually messy home with toys scattered here and there, and a jelly sandwich stuck in a corner of the carpet I rarely get to clean? Each day I search for little bits of God's holiness hidden in the mundane. It's these gifts that make up my main diet of praise. They become my bread-and-butter discoveries of his goodness.

So I thank him for the gifts I hear: Daddy humming to his daughter, the tiny snore of my sleeping baby, the squeaking chatter of Ginger our guinea pig, and the bubbles in our fish tank.

I thank him for the gifts I see: Chubby fingers capturing a potato bug in the wet garden, a tiny sprout from a seedling I didn't plant, my child mimicking motherhood with her baby doll.

And I thank God for the gifts I feel: The sticky jelly fingerprints on my blouse, the feel of dirty little hands under running water, the sloppy baby kiss on my mouth, the silky softness of my child's cheek on mine.

These gifts remind me that I'm not a prisoner of potty chairs and playthings. I'm free in Christ and I praise him for life. Each gift reminds me I praise a living God, a God full of life. For that, I'll break out the pots and pans and wooden spoons and open my window of praise.

DAY ONE

Key Verse: 1 Thessalonians 5:18 Give thanks in all circumstances, for this is God's will for you in Christ Jesus.

Key Thought: What circumstances make it most difficult for me to give thanks or praise God?

41

*Fish
Bubbles
and
Guinea
Pig
Chatter*

DAY TWO

Key Verse: Psalm 100:4–5 Enter his gates with thanksgiving and his courts with praise; give thanks to him and praise his name. For the LORD is good and his love endures forever; his faithfulness continues through all generations.

Key Thought: According to these verses, what are some reasons why I can praise God?

DAY THREE

Key Verse: Psalm 145:13 The LORD is faithful to all his promises and loving toward all he has made.

Key Thought: Read all of Psalm 145. What words in this chapter of praise comfort me? For which of the promises will I praise God?

DAY FOUR

Key Verse: Psalm 150:6 Let everything that has breath praise the LORD. Praise the LORD.

Key Thought: Psalm 150 reminds me I can be creative and diverse in how I praise God.

DAY FIVE

Key Verse: Psalm 69:34 Let heaven and earth praise him, the seas and all that move in them.

Key Thought: I will observe God's creation today and look for ways it praises him.

Day Six

Key Verse: Habakkuk 3:17–19 Though the fig tree does not bud and there are no grapes on the vines, though the olive crop fails and the fields produce no good, though there are no sheep in the pen and no cattle in the stalls, yet I will rejoice in the LORD, I will be joyful in God my Savior. The Sovereign LORD is my strength; he makes my feet like the feet of a deer, he enables me to go on the heights.

Key Thought: What assurances does God give me when I praise him in hard times?

Day Seven

Father of every good gift,
   I don't know how I get myself into
      such a sour disposition that I
become blind to the wonder and goodness
      you place right under my nose.
All too soon my little children will be grown and gone.
All I see as my chains today
      will turn to a mist of memories tomorrow.
Forgive my selfish heart for always wanting
      what I don't have

*Fish
Bubbles
and
Guinea
Pig
Chatter*

and regretting what I do have.
I'll begin today to brighten my world
     by opening a window of praise to you.
I praise the mighty works of your hands, seen in this
     tiny world shared by mother and child.

Amen.

To Do

1. Count your blessings. Number the lines on a sheet of paper and don't stop writing until the paper is full.
2. Teach your children to play "I spy" by asking them to be on the lookout with you for hidden gifts from God. Ask them as they go to bed, "Did you see God through his gifts today?" Help them keep a running list of the gifts they find from God.
3. Gifts from God don't always come in pretty wrapping. Ask God to reveal his gifts to you even in the midst of problems.

*Fish
Bubbles
and
Guinea
Pig
Chatter*

Fish Bubbles and Guinea Pig Chatter

4

More Water, Mom
Trusting Jesus

To be fully present where we are, to be fully keyed to what we are doing, frees us from servitude to the past and the harassment of the future. This day, this moment of time, is all that really concerns us.

Elizabeth Yates

I stared at the stack of bills piled high on my kitchen table just begging to be paid. The happy voices of my daughter, Megan, and her two visiting cousins pushed into my mind. I tapped the pen on top of the checkbook. I was feeling a bit ragged around the edges emotionally. I worried their laughter might wake little Amy, who had finally fallen asleep after fussing with an ear infection all morning.

Taking a deep breath, I opened the checkbook and braced myself to pay the bills. It hadn't been easy since my husband had been laid off and started his own consulting business during the last year. So I prayed, "Lord, get us through this first year—just one good year to get us on our feet. That's all I ask."

"Mom, we need more water and some lunch," came the call from the backyard. Amy woke and began to cry. I grabbed three paper cups and hastily filled them with water. "Here," I snapped as I delivered the water outside. Amy was nearly screaming now. "This is just too much, Lord. Please make her healthy again for both our sakes." I returned to the kitchen to stir a pot of soup with one hand. I tried to comfort Amy as she wiggled in my other arm.

"Mom, can we make a tent? Where's our lunch?" they continued to demand.

"I can't do everything at once," I hollered back over Amy's wail. As the soup simmered, I stared out the kitchen window rocking Amy back and forth, watching the children. They were digging up the dirt, throwing it in the air, feeling the goodness of the earth and sun and smiling at one another. A thought hit me, clear and fresh as mountain air:

They never ask for more than they need to get through any given moment. Their simple hearts trusted me enough to ask for only one meal at a time, or a small cup of water to quench their thirst.

I cringed as I considered the contrast between their free spirits and my fearful, worried mind. Moments before, I had asked God for assurances about our income for the entire year! I wanted good health for my family now and forevermore. Fairytale wishes of a life without problems clouded my communication with God. I call them "worry prayers." They're not really productive—just a righteous way to worry.

I groped for a mere memory of that worry-free childlike quality I saw in the kids out back. Then I remembered Christ's words to a very worried Martha, "You are worried and upset about many things, but only one thing is needed. Mary has chosen what is better, and it will not be taken away from her" (Luke 10:41–42). Mary's choice? To sit at the Lord's feet listening to what he said.

I called the kids in for lunch. Amy had fallen back asleep in my arms, and I thought, Jesus has enough to take care of all my needs, but he does it only as I choose moment by moment to trust him. For this moment, all I need is to sit down and listen.

DAY ONE

Key Verse: Hebrews 12:2–3 Let us fix our eyes on Jesus, the author and perfecter of our faith. . . . Consider him who endured such opposition from sinful men, so that you will not grow weary and lose heart.

Key Thought: What will happen when I stop at Jesus' feet to look at him and listen? What must I do to be able to hear Jesus?

DAY TWO

Key Verse: Luke 10:40 But Martha was distracted by all the preparations that had to be made. She came and asked, "Lord, don't you care that my sister has left me to do the work by myself? Tell her to help me."

Key Thought: What was Martha's real problem here? Do I have similar problems?

DAY THREE

Key Verse: Luke 12:22–25 Do not worry about your life, what you will eat; or about your body, what you will wear. Life is more than food, and the body more than clothes. Consider the ravens: They do not sow or reap, they have no storeroom or barn; yet God feeds them. And how much more valuable you are than birds! Who of you by worrying can add a single hour to his life? Since you cannot do this very little thing, why do you worry about the rest?

Key Thought: Why is it foolish for me to spend time worrying?

DAY FOUR

Key Verse: 1 Peter 5:7 Cast all your anxiety on him because he cares for you.

Key Thought: The simple truth is that I can stop worrying when I start believing Jesus cares for me.

DAY FIVE

Key Verse: Philippians 4:6–7 Do not be anxious about anything, but in everything, by prayer and petition, with thanksgiving, present your requests to God. And the peace of God, which transcends all understanding, will guard your hearts and your minds in Christ Jesus.

Key Thought: God promises if I give my cares to him he will bless me not with a problem-free life but with peace.

DAY SIX

Key Verse: John 16:33 "I have told you these things, so that in me you may have peace. In this world you will have trouble. But take heart! I have overcome the world."

Key Thought: The world offers me trouble, Jesus offers me peace. My choice is clear.

DAY SEVEN

Father of peace,

You want my worries to be your worries, my cares your cares.

Here you go. Take away the anxiety.

Let your Spirit of peace stand guard over my heart and mind to keep out future intruders who want to rob me of your love.

Amen.

TO DO

1. Notice each day if or when you hear your children worrying. If they do worry, how do you help them? Consider how much more God wants to help you as his child.

2. Make an honest evaluation of the amount of time you "sit and listen" to Jesus in prayer time, Bible study, being alone. Make a solid goal this week to develop a fresh approach to your personal time with Christ.

3. Read Matthew 6:25–34 through the week. How is Christ speaking to you through these words? What

is the most difficult portion of this Bible passage to apply to your life? Ask Jesus to open your eyes to fully comprehend his intent for you.

MY TURN

5

I Found a Golden Stone
Knowing Your Value to God

*God invented the universe to delight us . . . his love is so
much for each one alone that it seems as if the moon and stars
had been made for our nursery windows and no other crea-
ture had occupied God's mind since time began.*

Emilie Griffin

"**M**ommy, come see. I found a golden stone,"
Megan breathlessly called through the screen door. Thinking she had unearthed a piece of foil or a bit of glittery quartz,

55

I hurried to the back door to see. With a look of utter wonderment, she lifted the precious treasure in her chubby hands for me to have a closer look.

I took it and turned it over and over again hoping to find at least a flash of sparkle. With a bit of disappointment I realized she held nothing more than a mud-encrusted lump of broken cement. "I was digging in the dirt, and there it was—a whole piece of gold," she added in great excitement.

"Put it on my shelf with my 'breakable' things, Mommy." There it would join her other prized possessions: a pair of painted Dutch wooden shoes from a neighborhood garage sale, one broken-off deer antler Daddy found in the forest while hunting, and three tiny porcelain birthday dolls.

Just as Megan turned a seemingly worthless piece of dirt into an honored treasure, so Christ values me, broken and full of sin. This act of honor is simple enough for even a child to carry out quite naturally. But it's a hard task for me to see the beauty of my own restored soul when I harbor doubts about my own worth.

These self-doubts often poke up their ugly little heads following periods when I'm angry or disappointed by life: hearing of yet another marriage on the rocks, losing a job, a friend's death, or a simple misunderstanding. Burying my hurts deep in my heart makes it impossible to offer my whole heart to God. So I swim in the pity pool of insecurity and

wonder why I feel so worthless. And there I sulk. It's my way of hiding from God.

Hiding in my insecurities erodes my self-worth to the point of doubting God's ability to love me beyond my humanness. When I reach that point, I remind myself that, regardless of my own feelings, thoughts, or actions, God never withdraws his love from me.

So how do I throw off my grownup self-doubts, my moody, unlovable character, my defeatist attitudes? How do I make the transition of placing value and confidence back in my life? By replacing the lies of this world with God's true image of me—the one he created at the beginning of time—his own image.

Daily I must affirm in my heart that God doesn't love me only a little or only out of a godly obligation because of something I've done. He loves me without reservation. He loved me first. That love is meant to be savored and enjoyed by each of us. "How great is the love the Father has lavished on us, that we should be called children of God" (1 John 3:1).

It's time to let God pick me up and love me as I am, where I am, and for who I am. Because when he picks me up out of the dirt, I become to him as precious as gold. And if I listen closely enough, I'll hear him proclaim in breathless wonder, "My child."

DAY ONE

Key Verse: Psalm 103:11–13 For as high as the heavens are above the earth, so great is his love for those who fear him; as far as the east is from the west, so far has he removed our transgressions from us. As a father has compassion on his children, so the LORD has compassion on those who fear him.

Key Thought: This verse tells me of the extremities of God's love for me.

DAY TWO

Key Verse: Psalm 40:2 He lifted me out of the slimy pit, out of the mud and mire; he set my feet on a rock and gave me a firm place to stand.

Key Thought: This verse tells me that God wants to rescue me from my self-destructive view of myself.

DAY THREE

Key Verse: Romans 8:38–39 For I am convinced that neither death nor life, neither angels nor demons, neither the present nor the future, nor any powers, neither height nor depth, nor anything else in all creation, will be able to separate us from the love of God that is in Christ Jesus our Lord.

Key Thought: I can be completely confident in God's sure and eternal love of me.

59

DAY FOUR

Key Verse: Isaiah 61:10 I delight greatly in the LORD; my soul rejoices in my God. For he has clothed me with garments of salvation and arrayed me in a robe of righteousness.

Key Thought: According to this verse, God sees me as someone valued and precious to him.

DAY FIVE

Key Verse: Hosea 2:19–20 I will betroth you to me forever; I will betroth you in righteousness and justice, in love and compassion. I will betroth you in faithfulness, and you will acknowledge the LORD.

Key Thought: I know I am highly valued by God because I am constantly in his love.

DAY SIX

Key Verse: Ephesians 5:2 Live a life of love, just as Christ loved us and gave himself up for us as a fragrant offering and sacrifice to God.

Key Thought: If Christ loved me enough to become my sacrifice, I cannot help but be grateful and loving to him.

DAY SEVEN

I Found a Golden Stone

Father of all creation,
> I stand here broken by sin.
> Resentment and anger encrust my heart like dried mud.
> My thoughts weigh heavily
>   with boredom and worry and strife.
Father, cradle me in your strong hands.
Lift my soul from the miry clay.
Set me in a seat of high honor right next to Jesus,
Where you can see the gold in my life.
Look into my eyes and speak these miraculous words:
> "My child."

Amen.

TO DO

1. Choose one of the passages listed above and memorize the passage. This is God's promise to you.

2. Do something creative with your children (plant an herb garden, come up with a unique recipe, rearrange the furniture, start a diary). Now meditate on God's creativity in Genesis 1 and revel in the fact that he created you in his image.

3. Point out to your children the beauty of some ordinary or even ugly object of nature. Help them un-

61

derstand God sees the good in each of us when we
have Jesus in our hearts.

MY TURN

6

There's a Cricket in My Room
Finding God's Comfort

We may hope sometimes for little scraps of comfort. Why do
we run frightened away from the "all comfort" that is ours
in the salvation of the Lord Jesus Christ?

Hannah Smith

*W*ith terror in her eyes and horror in her voice,
Megan rounded the kitchen corner screaming, "There's a

kwicket in my woom!" She ran for dear life straight to Daddy. (She knows Mommy is not fond of the things either.) "Get it out!" she ordered.

"Okay. Let's go," Daddy said as they made their way to her bedroom. She stopped at the doorway and pointed inside. "There it is, Daddy." She released his hand to watch her brave warrior enter her worst nightmare.

With a shoe as his chosen weapon, he promptly squashed the intruder, picked it up with a tissue, went across the hall, and flushed it down. Turning to his little girl, he said, "There, it's all gone. You're safe now." She gave a big sigh and threw her arms around his neck in thanks.

My children know with uncanny clarity where to go when they need comfort. But often I seem to misplace the comfort and security only God gives. I begin to search, instead, in all the wrong places. Rather than run to God with my fears, my inadequacies, and my imperfections, I prop myself up with all sorts of false comfort. Some crutches are not only acceptable by the world's standards, they're even encouraged.

It's easy to hide behind a hectic schedule of work, play groups, or volunteer jobs. Better yet, why not avoid the hurt and find "comfort" in church activities? No one will ever suspect my fears there. But the comfort offered by this world is a tainted salve, serving only to damage more deeply.

My real comfort begins and ends with my heavenly father. Second Corinthians 1:3 tells us the father of compassion, the God of all comfort, comforts us in all our troubles. But how does he do it? The Greek word interpreted as "comfort" originally meant "to walk alongside of."

In other words, God doesn't offer a condescending comfort. He doesn't send me off with a pat on the head to do battle with my "crickets." God's comfort reaches my deepest need. He's right there with me walking through the trials. He's forging my path, slashing back the overgrowth.

I like Amy Carmichael's description: "He who begins, finishes. He who leads us on, follows behind to deal in love with our poor attempts. . . . He gathers up the things we have dropped—our fallen resolutions, our mistakes. . . . He makes His pardon to flow over our sins till they are utterly washed away. And He turns to fight the Enemy, who would pursue after us to destroy us from behind. *He is first and He is last!* And we are gathered up in between as in great arms of eternal lovingkindness."

When I turn to pray, "Come, walk with me, Father," and then listen for his footsteps, in that moment comes my comfort. It's as simple as a child trusting her daddy. God is always armed with comfort for his child. Then the Father of *all* compassion, the God of *all* comfort will come to me and walk alongside me.

DAY ONE

Key Verse: Psalm 119:50 My comfort in my suffering is this: Your promise preserves my life.

Key Thought: God's promises comfort me because when I'm afraid, he keeps me safe.

DAY TWO

Key Verse: Psalm 103:13 As a father has compassion on his children, so the LORD has compassion on those who fear him.

Key Thought: God's comfort, God's compassion is even more tender than a loving father comforting a hurt child.

DAY THREE

Key Verse: Isaiah 46:4 Even to your old age and gray hairs I am he, I am he who will sustain you. I have made you and I will carry you; I will sustain you and I will rescue you.

Key Thought: According to this verse, God's comfort picks me up, holds me, and saves me.

DAY FOUR

Key Verse: Isaiah 63:9 In all their distress he too was distressed, and the angel of his presence saved them. In his love

There's a Cricket in My Room

67

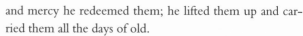

and mercy he redeemed them; he lifted them up and carried them all the days of old.

Key Thought: God walks with me and feels my distress, comforting me all the days of my life.

DAY FIVE

Key Verse: Isaiah 66:13 As a mother comforts her child, so will I comfort you.

Key Thought: God comforts me like my mother comforted me and as I comfort my children today.

DAY SIX

Key Verse: John 16:33 I have told you these things, so that in me you may have peace. In this world you will have trouble. But take heart! I have overcome the world.

Key Thought: One of God's greatest comforts lies in the fact that his love conquers all.

DAY SEVEN

Father of all compassion, God of all comfort,

How it hurts when insensitive words are shot my way! I cry for the sadness in this world, on my street. It all threatens to dismantle my peace. I feel like running to the nearest escape hatch offered by the world. But the hurt and sadness only return.

So I cry out to you.

Let your compassion for me and my world carry me through the tangles of pain. Comfort my crying heart. Come, walk with me today, Father.

Amen.

To Do

1. Determine ways you can offer God's comfort to others and then set a plan of action to carry out that comfort.

2. Take note of the times your children seek comfort from you. How do you respond? How does this help you to understand God's comfort?

3. Ask several other Christians how they have been comforted by God during trials in their lives. This will give you and them an opportunity to share your testimonies of God's work in your lives and help you to further understand the depth of God's comfort.

MY TURN

7

I'm Dumping My Cereal
Dealing with Discipline and Grace

I gladly accept that grace which makes me ever more humble, more reverent, and more ready to renounce self . . . give thanks to God for His grace, and confess that the guilt and penalty of sin are yours alone.

Thomas a'Kempis

*F*or a time, Megan's behavior seemed intolerable to me as she passed through that "limit testing" preschool age. She

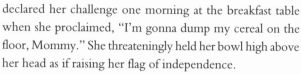

declared her challenge one morning at the breakfast table when she proclaimed, "I'm gonna dump my cereal on the floor, Mommy." She threateningly held her bowl high above her head as if raising her flag of independence.

"Remember what happens when you disobey. And you'll have to clean up the mess too," I reminded her calmly as I cooked eggs at the stove. She stopped to think a minute.

Then, as if to make an informed decision, she asked me to further define the boundaries I'd set. "Will I have to clean it up by myself, or will you help me?"

"If you make the mess, you clean it up by yourself," I confirmed.

Dealing with intolerable behavior can unnerve even the calmest parent. I am comforted, though, by the thought that God relates to my feelings as I discipline my children through each phase of their growth. In fact, as a parent, God himself faced blatant rebellion by his first children, Adam and Eve. Certainly their behavior could be labeled "intolerable," given the paradise they possessed. More to the point, what about me? Don't I continue on that same road of disobedience and, at times, outright rebellion when I try to hide behind my good works or blame someone else for my problems? Couldn't my behavior be labeled "intolerable," given God's gift of life coupled with his promises to comfort and love me?

God's methods of discipline are seen throughout Scripture with these characteristics: he sets limits; he reinforces the limits if necessary; he restores the relationship with his children over and over again. This is his grace. Adam and Eve lived in God's perfect creation. But before their sin, God had set the limits. "Don't eat from that tree," he told them. Unfortunately, they crossed over that boundary line, so God reinforced his boundary.

The saddest truth to this story is not that Adam and Eve disobeyed, but that they chose to separate themselves from God. Rather than run to him in their sin, they chose to hide, to blame, and to remain in control. A gaping hole remained. There was no sorrow for their sin—only an uncomfortable embarrassment over their condition. I have to believe God must have waited, like the father of the prodigal son, for his children to run to him.

Despite their rebellion, and despite their need to leave paradise, God's grace abounded. As Adam and Eve turned to leave, trying to hide themselves, their shame, and their sins, God stopped them. His discipline wasn't yet complete. Before he sent them out alone he explained to them how life would be from then on—what they could expect. He prepared them for their future. And then, with the tenderness of a loving father, he personally clothed them. He restored the relationship and began the grand design finally leading to Christ's sacrifice for their sin, the ultimate form of grace.

Without another word, Megan set down her bowl and finished her breakfast. Afterward I gave her a hug and told her I was proud of her for choosing to do the right thing. By loving my sometimes rebellious children I see the seemingly fathomless depth of my love is merely a wading pool compared with the ocean of God's love and grace for me. I think I'll forego the challenge of the cereal bowl today. I'll give God's grace a place in my heart instead.

I'm Dumping My Cereal

DAY ONE

Key Verse: Hebrews 12:11 No discipline seems pleasant at the time, but painful. Later on, however, it produces a harvest of righteousness and peace for those who have been trained by it.

Key Thought: If I accept God's discipline, his righteousness and peace will be seen in my life.

DAY TWO

Key Verse: 2 Corinthians 4:17–18 For our light and momentary troubles are achieving for us an eternal glory that far outweighs them all. So we fix our eyes not on what is seen, but on what is unseen. For what is seen is temporary, but what is unseen is eternal.

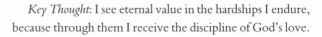

Key Thought: I see eternal value in the hardships I endure, because through them I receive the discipline of God's love.

DAY THREE

Key Verse: Revelation 3:19–20 Those whom I love I rebuke and discipline. So be earnest and repent. Here I am! I stand at the door and knock. If anyone hears my voice and opens the door, I will come in and eat with him, and he with me.

Key Thought: What response does Jesus expect from me after I've been disciplined? How will he restore our relationship?

DAY FOUR

Key Verse: Proverbs 3:11–12 My son, do not despise the LORD's discipline and do not resent his rebuke, because the LORD disciplines those he loves, as a father the son he delights in.

Key Thought: God's discipline proves his love for me.

DAY FIVE

Key Verse: Deuteronomy 8:3 He humbled you, causing you to hunger and then feeding you with manna, which neither you nor your fathers had known, to teach you that man does not live on bread alone but on every word that comes from the mouth of the LORD.

Key Thought: When God disciplines me, he never fails to comfort me as well.

DAY SIX

Key Verse: 2 Corinthians 9:8 And God is able to make all grace abound to you, so that in all things at all times, having all that you need, you will abound in every good work.

Key Thought: Regardless of my abilities or inabilities, God's grace is all I will ever need.

DAY SEVEN

Abba, Father,

When life seems hard and the temptations strong, I ponder whether it would be easier for me just to "jump the fence."

But then you remind me it's not until I've passed through the fire that I can turn to see the refined gold. Then I know your discipline was good and right. By it you prepare me, strengthen me, lead me, love me into what I can become.

In the worst way I need your grace and seek your mercy.

In the best way you grant it without hesitation.

I'm Dumping My Cereal

Steady me to face the next challenge of life and to know your discipline is filled with love.

Amen.

To Do

1. As you discipline your child (teach your child), consider how your discipline is similar to God's. How does it differ?

2. Ask God specifically to unveil the hidden areas of disobedience in your life. Then ask him to melt it all away by the warmth of his grace. Affirm his action by memorizing 2 Corinthians 9:8.

3. Look up the word *discipline* in the dictionary and Bible concordance. What positive connotations does this word carry? How can you integrate these meanings into your interaction with your child?

*I'm
Dumping
My
Cereal*

I'm Dumping My Cereal

MY TURN

80

8

Look, Mommy, No Mud

Finding God's Forgiveness

Some men are only virtuous enough to forget that they are sinners without being wretched enough to remember how much they need the mercy of God.

Thomas Merton

*O*ne day I caught my daughter "mud-handed" squishing and squashing in the goop made from a dripping garden

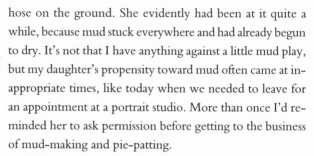

Look Mommy, No Mud

hose on the ground. She evidently had been at it quite a while, because mud stuck everywhere and had already begun to dry. It's not that I have anything against a little mud play, but my daughter's propensity toward mud often came at inappropriate times, like today when we needed to leave for an appointment at a portrait studio. More than once I'd reminded her to ask permission before getting to the business of mud-making and pie-patting.

"What have you been doing?" I demanded, my hands on my hips.

"I'm building a road," she explained in all seriousness.

"But I just cleaned you up. Look at the mess you've made. There's mud everywhere!" She looked at her hands and then her clothes as if she hadn't noticed them before. Then she looked at me and began to cry.

I picked her up and brought her in. I started scrubbing and rubbing with soap and water. She protested, but finally the dirt disappeared and she smelled sweet and clean again. Once the washing stopped, I wrapped her up in a warm, soft towel. The complaining ceased and we snuggled together.

The following day, she was eager to go out to play again. "The mud is off limits," I reminded. Later she came skipping in with hands held high. "Look, Mommy. No mud today," she said proudly. I hugged her and said, "I'm so

happy when you want to obey. That's how I know you love me."

I get caught "mud-handed" too when I play with what seems as innocent as a few drops of water in the dirt. I slip out of the habit of church attendance to sleep in; I can't find time to read my Bible but always seem to squeeze in the latest issue of *People*; I choose another route for my evening walk rather than pass the talkative old woman down the street. Before long, I haven't merely jumped out of God's arms to frolic at his feet. I've run far away and fallen facedown in the mud. But a good shepherd always finds his lost sheep and mends it and washes it when necessary.

So I ask for the soap by repenting and seeking God's mercy. I get scrubbed clean by claiming the cleansing power of Christ's blood. I wrap up in a warm towel by letting God reassure me of his love through Scripture.

But for me, the hardest step is to be like a child, always ready to go and try again. God wants me to be ready to walk in his will and answer his call again, even after I've failed him in the worst way. Imagine if children stopped growing, stopped playing, stopped being children simply because they broke a rule. The point to God's forgiveness is to make me willing and able to do what I was created to do.

When I take the soap and water and wash at God's fountain of forgiveness, then I can run to my Father with hands held high and clean, and proudly say, "Look, Daddy. No mud today."

DAY ONE

Key Verse: Deuteronomy 26:17–18 You have declared this day that the LORD is your God and that you will walk in his ways, that you will keep his decrees, commands and laws, and that you will obey him. And the LORD has declared this day that you are his people, his treasured possession as he promised, and that you are to keep all his commands.

Key Thought: When I choose to walk in God's way by "staying out of the mud," he claims me as his treasured possession.

DAY TWO

Key Verse: Isaiah 1:18–19 "Come now, let us reason together," says the LORD. "Though your sins are like scarlet, they shall be as white as snow; though they are red as crimson, they shall be like wool. If you are willing and obedient, you will eat the best from the land."

Key Thought: God wants to change my stained heart by removing my sin and making my heart anew.

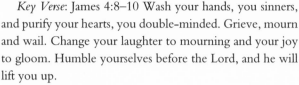

*Look
Mommy,
No Mud*

DAY THREE

Key Verse: James 4:8–10 Wash your hands, you sinners, and purify your hearts, you double-minded. Grieve, mourn and wail. Change your laughter to mourning and your joy to gloom. Humble yourselves before the Lord, and he will lift you up.

Key Thought: Why must I experience grief, mourning, and gloom to be forgiven?

DAY FOUR

Key Verse: Mark 1:40–41 A man with leprosy came to him and begged him on his knees, "If you are willing, you can make me clean." Filled with compassion, Jesus reached out his hand and touched the man. "I am willing," he said. "Be clean!"

Key Thought: Disobedience followed by forgiveness compares to this man's physical cleansing in that Jesus' sacrifice and cleansing came out of his compassion for sinners.

DAY FIVE

Key Verse: Matthew 23:25 You clean the outside of the cup and dish, but inside they are full of greed and self-indulgence. Blind Pharisee! First clean the inside of the cup and dish, and then the outside also will be clean.

Key Thought: My good works do not hide my inner sin.

DAY SIX

Key Verse: Psalm 24:3–5 Who may ascend the hill of the
LORD? Who may stand in his holy place? He who has clean
hands and a pure heart. . . . He will receive blessing from
the LORD.

Key Thought: It's important for me to be clean and pure
before God because God is holy.

DAY SEVEN

Lord of all mercy,

I get so carried away by my sin that soon I'm covered with mud from head to toe. Stop me, Lord, before I fall completely into the mud puddle again. Stop
me and tell me to "look at this mess!"

Then I'll come with you willingly to let you wash
me clean, because I long for the moment when you
wrap me in your loving arms again.

Amen.

TO DO

1. Stop using past sin as a guilt trip. List three ways God
   can use your healing and forgiveness in a positive way
   as a tool of ministry for someone else.

*Look
Mommy,
No Mud*

87

*Look
Mommy,
No Mud*

2. Use bath time with the kids as an opportunity to talk with them about how Jesus makes us clean inside too.
3. Read Psalm 51 in its entirety as a prayer for forgiveness and healing in your life.

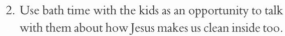

MY TURN

9

Come On In, Mommy
Making God Lord of All

Do you think of your holy heavenly Father as you would an addition on a house?—an improvement to an already existing structure? I am your life. I'll have nothing less than your life from you.

Marie Chapian

*C*ome on, Mommy," my girls cried. They were splashing in the pool with Daddy.

"No, that's okay. I'll just watch in the shade."

Amazingly, the midday heat on a Phoenix summer afternoon made even 85 degree water feel like ice. I had no desire to brave the shock of jumping in. Besides, I had my glass of iced tea and had dipped my towel in the pool to keep close at hand should I begin to overheat.

Sitting in the shade, my mind drifted to thoughts of how my relationship with God had changed over the past several months. During this time God had seemed light years away. I wasn't going through any particular hardship. I hadn't neglected my prayer life or Bible reading. I even kept a journal of my spiritual journey. So why did I feel as though I was knocking at heaven's door but no one was home? I knew how the psalmist felt when he said, "When you hid your face, I was dismayed" (Ps. 30:7).

But the days of God's silence turned into weeks and weeks into months until I was nearly frantic with my effort to find out why God had moved and left no forwarding address. While I was praying for God to be a part of my life again, I was struck by a passage of Scripture: "Become mature, attaining to the *whole* measure of the fullness of Christ" (Eph. 4:13, emphasis added). How could I get a whole measure of Christ when I continued to ask for only a small portion of him. I had used him, like a towel dipped in the water, for my own comfort and needs at my convenience.

Certain parts of my life I kept under my own tight control rather than entrust them to Christ. My writing had taken precedence over my growth in God. And I held so tightly to my poor eating habits that my knuckles ached from the grip on this "pleasure." But my prayers for deliverance or quick fixes didn't bring the answers I wanted. I was like Naaman in the Old Testament.

Naaman had leprosy and wanted a cure. A servant of the prophet Elisha told him to go dip seven times in the Jordan River for God's healing. Naaman was downright insulted because the old prophet himself would not attend to him. Couldn't Elisha wave his hands a few times and heal Naaman? God was not meeting Naaman's expectations! But it wasn't Naaman's leprosy that needed the healing. His need to control and be catered to had become the false god he worshiped (2 Kings 5:1–14).

A spiritual sickness had eaten away at my heart like a leprosy. But I wasn't willing to take God's whole antidote either. I wanted God to meet my terms, which meant to let me control what I wanted to control. I didn't think I needed to dip *seven* times when I could just dip my towel to comfort myself.

So I confessed to God I didn't want only a part of him anymore. I wanted to immerse myself wholly in him. I was tired of lying at the edge of the pool. It was time to splash and squeal and dive in like my children, even if diving in meant looking at some painful areas in my life. God's answer wasn't quick and miraculous. At his own speed God started healing me of deeply ingrained dependencies on earthly comforts. But this time I was ready and willing to begin the whole treatment.

The laughter and pool play sent water splashing on my hot skin, and I jumped. I was ready to join in the fun. "Look out," I called. "I'm jumping in!"

DAY ONE

Key Verse: Romans 14:8 If we live, we live to the Lord; and if we die, we die to the Lord. So, whether we live or die, we belong to the Lord.

Key Thought: Christ's lordship is all encompassing. From the breath I breathe to my dying thoughts, Jesus is Lord.

DAY TWO

Key Verse: Psalm 86:11 Teach me your way, O LORD, and I will walk in your truth; give me an undivided heart, that I may fear your name.

Key Thought: What areas of my heart remain divided between God and other priorities?

DAY THREE

Key Verse: Ezekiel 11:19 I will give them an undivided heart and put a new spirit in them; I will remove from them their heart of stone and give them a heart of flesh.

Key Thought: When I ask God to give me a heart of flesh, I'm asking him to help me to be a vital person, receptive and sensitive to God's Spirit as the source and guide of my life.

DAY FOUR

Key Verse: 2 Corinthians 5:15 And he died for all, that those who live should no longer live for themselves but for him who died for them and was raised again.

Key Thought: When I make Christ Lord of my life, I can expect to see all parts of my life in their proper perspective.

DAY FIVE

Key Verse: Galatians 2:20 I have been crucified with Christ and I no longer live, but Christ lives in me. The life I live in the body, I live by faith in the Son of God, who loved me and gave himself for me.

Key Thought: When I bury my desire to control my problems, I can trust Christ to bring new life because he is faithful to love me through it all.

Day Six

Key Verse: Luke 21:4 All these people gave their gifts out of their wealth; but she out of her poverty put in all she had to live on.

Key Thought: The only way to make God Lord of all is to give him my all.

Come On In, Mommy

Day Seven

Lord of all, Lord of my being,

You know how I struggle to give you my all. And other days, after you've carried my load, I snatch it out of your hands and hoard it like a selfish, spoiled child.

Oh, to know the unceasing rest you offer when I lay down my burdens at your feet. Help me moment by moment to trust you to handle them better, to handle them all, in your way and time.

Amen.

To Do

1. Spend time today giving your children opportunities to talk to God. Listen to how they give their all to him—from the tiniest scratch to the neighbor's lost dog. Let them teach you who is Lord.

2. Express your willingness to make God Lord of your life by telling a friend about your decision and your struggles, or by writing a letter to God.

3. List the areas of your life in which you feel you are out of control (finances, eating, TV viewing, housekeeping). That out-of-control feeling may be the first sign you are trying to be in control rather than Christ. Ask him how he wants you to handle it, what he specifically wants you to do.

4. Read the classic book *In His Steps*, by Charles Sheldon.

MY TURN

Come
On In,
Mommy

*Come
On In,
Mommy*

10

It Stinks in the Kitchen
Learning through Disappointments

We look for visions from heaven, for earthquakes and thunders of God's power . . . and we never dream that all the time God is in the commonplace things and people around us. If we will do the duty that lies nearest, we shall see Him.

Oswald Chambers

*I*t was one of those mornings. As I hung up the phone after talking with the air conditioner repairman, my girls came running, excitement in their eyes. "Mommy, come and see. It stinks in the kitchen!" I ran after them and heard gurgling sounds before rounding the corner. Greeted by a wave of foul-smelling garbage, I stared in disbelief. Dirty water from the garbage disposal gently cascaded into the sink, over the counter, and now formed pools of yuk on my kitchen floor. It threatened to find its way to the carpeted dining room within minutes.

My girls jumped up and down at the prospect of their own indoor pool. "Can we get in it, Mommy, pleeeeease?"

"No!" I snapped, my nerves becoming oversensitive to another unneeded problem. Somehow I managed to keep those four little feet from diving into the middle of it all. With the girls sent off to play at the neighbor's, and my husband off to work, I began cleanup duty. With a sigh I said, "Lord, this isn't exactly what I had in mind when I quit my job to be at home with my kids."

The sad fact was that this reality of backed-up sinks, energetic children, and the never-ending clean-up duty didn't stretch quite far enough to meet my expectation of the perfect homemaker. All in all, I was one unhappy woman. I cried to God, "I hate this! I hate this feeling, this place, this mess. Give me back my joy." Somehow, after shaking that wet rag at God, I knew he just wanted me to get through it.

Mary and Martha didn't get what they expected either when their brother, Lazarus, had become ill and died. They

had put every ounce of their faith in Jesus. He had healed so many strangers, surely he would come to save one whom he loved like a brother. The sisters wept bitter tears. The unexpected loss of Lazarus shattered their hearts. But could they bear a betrayal by Jesus—the one who claimed to be their friend, the very Son of God?

Then Jesus came, and Jesus wept.

Mary and Martha both ran to meet him. They unloaded their disappointment at his feet. "If only you had been here." *If only.* The essence of all disappointment lay in those two little words.

Now Martha found it hard to trust Jesus when he ordered the stone taken away from the grave. "You can't open the grave, Lord," she protested. "He's been dead four days, and there's a bad odor."

But Jesus reassured her. "Did I not tell you that if you believed, you would see the glory of God?"

I picked up the mop and began again. "I got the message, Lord." There was, indeed, a bad odor to deal with, and it wasn't all coming from my kitchen. I caught a glimpse of my own entombed heart, foul smelling and overflowing with disappointments and failures.

But then, Jesus came. He stood right there with me as I mopped up the mess. There in my kitchen Jesus began to push away my stone of disappointment. I protested at first. "It's been so long, and there's a bad odor."

But he simply said, "If you believe, you will see the glory of God." His reassurance shattered that stone of disappointment, and new life began to emerge. An excitement rose inside me which I hadn't felt in nearly eighteen months.

The repairman came and fixed the air conditioner. My future at home with my girls and even the disasters shone with a new hope. The garbage that floats into my kitchen or my life holds no power over me. Now I know, even on "one of those days," I can see the glory of God.

DAY ONE

Key Verse: Romans 5:5 And hope does not disappoint us, because God has poured out his love into our hearts by the Holy Spirit whom he has given us.

Key Thought: The best thing for me to do when I'm disappointed is grasp for my gift of hope and believe I will see God's glory.

DAY TWO

Key Verse: Psalm 22:5 They cried to you and were saved; in you they trusted and were not disappointed.

Key Thought: The one thing that will never disappoint me is God's steadfast and saving love.

DAY THREE

Key Verse: Exodus 6:7a, 9 "I will take you as my own people, and I will be your God." . . . Moses reported this to the Israelites, but they did not listen to him because of their discouragement and cruel bondage.

Key Thought: What effect can discouragement have on me?

DAY FOUR

Key Verse: Numbers 32:9 After they went up to the Valley of Eshcol and viewed the land, they discouraged the Israelites from entering the land the LORD had given them.

Key Thought: What outside forces tempt me to succumb to discouragement?

DAY FIVE

Key Verse: Deuteronomy 1:21 See, the LORD your God has given you the land. Go up and take possession of it as the LORD, the God of your fathers, told you. Do not be afraid, do not be discouraged.

Key Thought: When I trust God rather than live in disappointment I am able to do what he calls me to do for others and for him.

It Stinks in the Kitchen

DAY SIX

Key Verse: 1 Chronicles 28:20 Be strong and courageous, and do the work. Do not be afraid or discouraged, for the LORD, my God, is with you. He will not fail you or forsake you until all the work for the service of the temple of the LORD is finished.

Key Thought: I can overcome discouragement or disappointments because God is with me and God is my strength.

DAY SEVEN

Glorious Father,

I'm not doing what I thought I could do with my life. I don't feel the way I thought I would feel. I'm having to look again and reconsider who I am. My heart feels as heavy as a wet mop when I contemplate the what-ifs and if-onlys of my life.

So I'm looking to you. Teach me to be content, whatever my circumstances may be. And tell me once again, despite my disappointments or disasters, "If you only believe, you'll see my glory."

Amen.

It Stinks in the Kitchen

To Do

1. Read Colossians 3:21. Take note of ways you may have discouraged or disappointed your children. What was their reaction? How do you encourage them?

2. List any regrets or unmet expectations in your life. Ask God how he wants you to handle each one, such as make amends, try again, forget the past.

3. Remember others who are dealing with disappointment. Find a way to encourage them with a phone call, a visit, a card, or a small gift.

My Turn

*It Stinks
in the
Kitchen*

MY TURN

11

Don't Let Go
Embracing Courage

When we find ourselves in situations that seem beyond our limits (actually we should look for such situations!), we must not hesitate because we feel inadequate. We must not complain about our limited resources. God tells us he is glorified in our weakness. God's Spirit will take and multiply what we have.

Rebecca Pippert

*Y*ou can do it. Just keep going. Pedal hard." I whispered encouragement in my daughter's ear as I ran be-

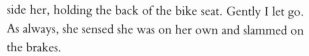

side her, holding the back of the bike seat. Gently I let go. As always, she sensed she was on her own and slammed on the brakes.

"Don't let go!" she ordered.

"But you can do it. I'm right beside you if you fall."

"But don't let go!" she insisted. "I can't do it." Would she ever have the confidence to master those two wheels?

Her words echoed in my ears. I've used the same feeble excuse more than I like to admit when I've spoken with God. "I can't do it, Lord." But he and I both know those excuses are nothing more than fear.

"I can't lose weight. I've tried it a hundred times before." (Fear translation: I'm afraid I might fail again.)

"I can't invite them over. The house is a wreck, and the furniture more than worn." (Fear translation: I'm afraid I won't be good enough for them.)

"I can't confront my husband about that. It'll only make things worse." (Fear translation: I'm afraid he'll reject me.)

The list is a mile long. Just like Moses, I run down my fear checklist to get out of a job I know God has called me to do. Exodus 3 and 4 records Moses' list of excuse after excuse: "I have no reputation; I have no authority; I'm not skilled in that area; I just don't want to do it; send someone else."

Don't
Let Go

But after each excuse, after he named each weakness and fear, Moses ran headlong into God's strength. God's response: "You have no reputation, but 'I AM.' You have no authority, but go in my name; 'I AM' has sent you. You have no skill, so I equip you with a mouthpiece. You have no desire, so I'll give you my power."

Why do I fear my weakness when God promises his strength in its place to fill in my blanks? My daughter eventually put down her excuses and said one morning, "I think I can ride, Mom." She chose to trust the courage and strength I had whispered in her ear. She went out, got on that bike, and rode down the street on her own.

God waits for me to trust his courage. I hear him whisper, "Go far in my strength; seize the opportunities with my power; make the most of what you're given in my grace." I can stop making excuses for my weakness. I've run headlong into the strength of the great I AM.

DAY ONE

Key Verse: Jeremiah 29:11 "For I know the plans I have for you," declares the LORD, "plans to prosper you and not to harm you, plans to give you hope and a future."

Key Thought: God wants me to let go of my fears and excuses so I can go forward in the hope he has for me.

DAY TWO

Key Verse: Colossians 1:29 To this end I labor, struggling with all his energy, which so powerfully works in me.

Key Thought: When I struggle with fears and weaknesses, I need to remember I have God's energy working for me.

DAY THREE

Key Verse: Exodus 4:10 Moses said to the LORD, "O Lord, I have never been eloquent, neither in the past nor since you have spoken to your servant. I am slow of speech and tongue."

Key Thought: What are some of the excuses I make to avoid the things I fear?

DAY FOUR

Key Verse: 2 Corinthians 13:4 For to be sure, he was crucified in weakness, yet he lives by God's power. Likewise, we are weak in him, yet by God's power we will live with him to serve you.

Key Thought: If Christ put his weakness in God's hands and received God's power, then I can do the same.

113

DAY FIVE

Key Verse: Romans 8:26 In the same way, the Spirit helps us in our weakness. We do not know what we ought to pray for, but the Spirit himself intercedes for us with groans that words cannot express.

Key Thought: When I'm too weak even to see the weakness and pray about it, I know that God's Spirit will do it for me.

DAY SIX

Key Verse: Romans 8:37 In all these things we are more than conquerors through him who loved us.

Key Thought: I can conquer any weakness only by doing it through Christ and his love.

DAY SEVEN

Lord of strength, omnipotent Father,

Opportunities are within my grasp every moment of my day. But instead of taking hold of the blessing of obedience, I too often remain frozen in fear, not risking, not trusting, not knowing how much goodness has my name written on it.

So with the light of your love, melt my fears away in your strength. Honor my feeble attempts as I reach out to you. Thank you for the gains I have made through your grace.

Amen.

Don't Let Go

To Do

1. Identify some of your personal weaknesses or fears. Ask God specifically what he wants you to do about them, or how he wants to use them for his glory.
2. When your child seems fearful, how do you help? How does this relate to God's view of your weakness?
3. Reread the quotation at the beginning of this chapter. Then ask yourself, What situations seem beyond my limits and capabilities? Do I find myself avoiding those situations?

My Turn

Don't
Let Go

MY TURN

12

But I Want It Now
Accepting What I'm Given

*Sometimes people speak of God having answered their prayer,
but what they mean is that He has answered it according to
their desire and done something about which they are glad.*

Amy Carmichael

"Mommy, can I have this candy?" Amy asked with
longing eyes.

"Not now. Dinner's almost ready."

"But I want it now."

117

"I know you want it now, but it will spoil your dinner, and you won't be a strong healthy girl if you don't eat good food," I explained with a smile.

She set the candy on the kitchen counter and waited at the table for her meal.

My prayers to God in days past had sounded like Amy's request. "Father, can I have a little more excitement and challenge in my life? Can't I spend one day with a good book without being interrupted at every fifth word? Do I have to do another load of laundry? I'm tired of picking up dirty socks."

The problem is, when there's still laundry piling up and constant interruptions, I don't "go to the table to wait for my meal." I assume God didn't hear me correctly, so I begin again but whine a little more loudly. Why don't I just listen to his answer and obey? I assume that because he didn't grant my wish like a genie in a lamp, he must not have heard. But if there's still laundry to do and little challenge on the horizon, then he *has* answered my prayer. He has told me, "No. Giving you what you selfishly want will ruin my plan for you in the long run."

I went through days and months wondering, "Where is the good in what I'm doing? I feel as though I'm withering away in these household routines." I had developed a resentment over doing the work God had given me. I found

little joy in caring for my family. Every call for "Mommy" felt like an interruption to every other task I started. And all I accomplished in the morning needed to be redone by afternoon.

So I began to pray over each task, each interruption. And I began to see his good purpose for me right now. Who is in a better position than a mother to learn what it means to be selfless, to die to your own desires so others may find joy? Who is better qualified to say, "This housework is so dull, my only joy is in doing it for God"? Who needs to learn such lessons more than I do? I realize it's easy to say, "Jesus is Lord of my life." But it takes a much greater commitment to say, "Jesus is Lord of this minute, Lord of my marriage, my relationships, Lord of my eating, Lord of my parenting, even Lord of my housekeeping." The more I seek his mercy and grace, the more I'm able to thank him for what he has given me and where he has placed me. And the more I thank him, the more I see him in my home, my marriage, my family. And the more I see him, the more I desire him.

DAY ONE

Key Verse: 2 Peter 1:5–8 Make every effort to add to your faith goodness; and to goodness, knowledge; and to knowledge, self-control; and to self-control, perseverance; and to perseverance, godliness; and to godliness, brotherly kindness; and to brotherly kindness; love. For if you possess these qualities in increasing measure, they will keep you from being ineffective and unproductive in your knowledge of our Lord Jesus Christ.

Key Thought: By seeking God in faith, he will grow me into an effective, productive servant for him.

DAY TWO

Key Verse: Revelation 2:10 Be faithful, even to the point of death, and I will give you the crown of life.

Key Thought: I can be faithful in making Christ Lord of all of my life, with his help.

DAY THREE

Key Verse: 2 Corinthians 10:5 We demolish arguments and every pretension that sets itself up against the knowledge of God, and we take captive every thought to make it obedient to Christ.

Key Thought: To make Christ Lord of my "minutes" I must, through my continuing study of Scripture, know what he wants me to be for him and his children.

DAY FOUR

Key Verse: Philippians 4:11–13 I have learned to be content whatever the circumstances. I know what it is to be in need, and I know what it is to have plenty. I have learned the secret of being content in any and every situation, whether well fed or hungry, whether living in plenty or in want. I can do everything through him who gives me strength.

Key Thought: The secret to contentment with Christ is to trust in his strength and love.

DAY FIVE

Key Verse: Hebrews 12:1b Let us throw off everything that hinders and the sin that so easily entangles, and let us run with perseverance the race marked out for us.

Key Thought: What race has Christ asked me to enter? How can I prepare for and run the best race for him?

DAY SIX

Key Verse: Philippians 3:7 But whatever was to my profit I now consider loss for the sake of Christ.

Key Thought: How can the things I consider profitable or good in my life be a loss to me or a detriment to my relationship with Christ?

DAY SEVEN

Father who hears my cry,

Forgive my presumption that because I know you I'll get my way. Forgive my arrogance that claims to hold your love when life is easy but assumes you're hiding when the going gets rough.

Give me wisdom to understand when you say no, and a heart filled with thanks because you always hear my prayer.

Amen.

But I Want It Now

TO DO

1. Identify any areas of your life which you continually ask God to change. Is it possible he has already given you the answer?

2. Describe your child's reaction when you do not allow him to do what he wants to do, even though what he wants is harmful to him. How does this parallel your reaction to God's answer to you?

3. List any benefits you have received or hope to receive through past or present difficult circumstances.

*But
I Want
It Now*

MY TURN

Epilogue

*T*he time with little ones at my feet is passing all too quickly. I began this "treasure hunt" with mere babes in my arms. By the time this book finds its way to your hands, Amy will be five years old and Megan nearly nine. But I know as they grow, new messages holding refreshing truths from God will continue to fill my treasure chest.

I remain convinced that "treasure hunting" is an art all mothers must cultivate and refine in their own way. In the brief description of Jesus' childhood found in Luke 2, twice it's recorded that Mary "treasured up all these things and pondered them in her heart." She knew she had much to learn from her child too.

My children teach me well. My treasure chest is full of spiritual jewels—jewels God personally hands to my daughters for special delivery into my life. How honored and

Epilogue

blessed I am that God chose me to be the caretaker of his little jewel bearers!

So I stand in wonder and anticipation of each day he grants me to be with my children. My prayer as their mother is this:

Lord, give me childlike eyes to see my children holding out your treasures to me each day. Give me childlike ears to hear your footsteps as they approach me in their need. Give me childlike hands, ready freely to give and receive your gifts. Teach me, Father, through my children, not in spite of them, how always to be your child.

Notes

CHAPTER 1

Henri Nouwen, *The Genesee Diary* (Garden City, N.Y.: Doubleday Image Books, 1981), 175.

CHAPTER 2

Mother Teresa, *Jesus, The Word to Be Spoken* (Ann Arbor, Mich.: Servant Books, 1986), 38.

CHAPTER 3

Sue Monk Kidd, *God's Joyful Surprise* (San Francisco: Harper & Row, 1987), 143.

CHAPTER 4

Elizabeth Yates, quoted in *Journeying Through the Days* (Nashville: The Upper Room, 1990).

CHAPTER 5

Emilie Griffin, *Clinging* (New York: McCracken Press, 1994), 94.

Notes

CHAPTER 6

Hannah Smith, quoted in *Safe Within Your Love* (Minneapolis: Bethany House Publishers, 1992), 104.

Amy Carmichael, quoted in *You Are My Hiding Place* (Minneapolis: Bethany House Publishers, 1991), 125.

CHAPTER 7

Thomas a'Kempis, *The Imitation of Christ* (London, England: Penguin Books, 1952), 81.

CHAPTER 8

Thomas Merton, *No Man Is an Island* (New York: Harcourt Brace Jovanovich, Publishers, 1955), 209.

CHAPTER 9

Marie Chapian, *His Gifts to Me* (Minneapolis: Bethany House Publishers, 1988), 36.

CHAPTER 10

Oswald Chambers, *My Utmost for His Highest* (Westwood, N.J.: Barbour and Company, Inc., 1935), 38.

CHAPTER 11

Rebecca Pippert, *Out of the Saltshaker and Into the World* (Downers Grove, Ill.: InterVarsity Press, 1979), 106.

CHAPTER 12

Amy Carmichael, *Thou Givest . . . They Gather* (Fort Washington, Penn.: Christian Literature Crusade, 1958), 52.